My Science Library

Zap!
It's Electricity!

by Buffy Silverman

Science Content Editor:
Kristi Lew

ROURKE CLASSROOM

www.rourkeclassroom.com

Science content editor: Kristi Lew

A former high school teacher with a background in biochemistry and more than 10 years of experience in cytogenetic laboratories, Kristi Lew specializes in taking complex scientific information and making it fun and interesting for scientists and non-scientists alike. She is the author of more than 20 science books for children and teachers.

www.rourkeclassroom.com

Photo credits: Cover © Jose Ignacio Soto, Cover logo frog © Eric Pohl, test tube © Sergey Lazarev; Table Of Contents © Carsten Reisinger; Page 4 © Monkey Business Images; Page 5 © Jill Battaglia; Page 7 © Wavebreakmedia Ltd; Page 8 © Darryl Vest; Page 9 © yui; Page 11 © Stephen Bures; Page 13 © Sky Light Pictures; Page 15 © Lisa F. Young; Page 17 © Konstantin Kirillov; Page 19 © nikkytok; Page 21 © Picsfive, James Hoenstine

Editor: Kelli Hicks

My Science Library series produced for Rourke by Blue Door Publishing, Florida

Library of Congress Cataloging-in-Publication Data

Silverman, Buffy.
Zap! it's electricity! / Buffy Silverman.
    p. cm. -- (My science library)
Includes bibliographical references and index.
ISBN 978-1-61741-753-5 (Hard cover) (alk. paper)
ISBN 978-1-61741-955-3
1. Electricity--Juvenile literature. I. Title. II. Series.

QC527.2.S54 2012
537--dc22

2011004838

Rourke Publishing
Printed in China, Voion Industry
  Guangdong Province
042011
042011LP

www.rourkeclassroom.com - rourke@rourkepublishing.com
Post Office Box 643328 Vero Beach, Florida 32964

Table of Contents

What Is Electricity?

Every day, we use **electricity**. Electricity powers the lights in our homes and schools. Computers, music players, cell phones, and refrigerators run on electricity.

How many ways do you use electricity?

5

Electricity helps keep our homes comfortable. In the summer, we use electricity to cool the air. We heat our homes with electricity in winter. Think of all the ways you use electricity at home.

If your video game is plugged in, it's using electricity. Even if you're not playing it!

Electricity provides the **energy** that people use every day. Energy is the ability to do **work**. We need energy to move objects, and to make heat, light, and sound. Electricity helps people do work.

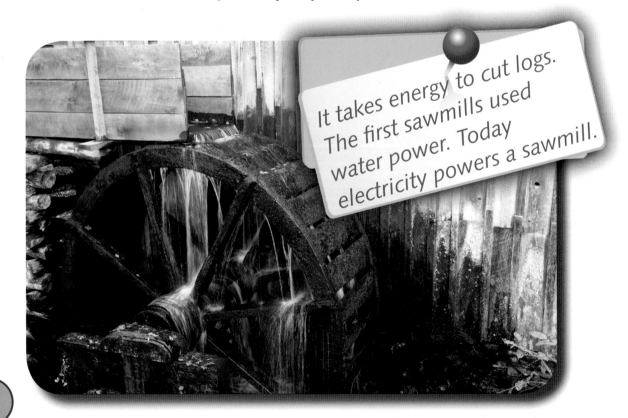

It takes energy to cut logs. The first sawmills used water power. Today electricity powers a sawmill.

Making Electricity

Power plants make electricity from different kinds of energy sources. Some power plants use wind, water, or solar power to make electricity. Other plants burn fuels like coal and natural gas to make electricity.

Wind turbines use the energy from moving air to make electricity.

Electricity flows through **power lines** made of metal. Metal wires are called **conductors**. They carry electricity. They bring electricity from a power plant to homes and other buildings.

Electricity may travel for many miles before it reaches your home.

Electric wires run inside the walls of your home. The outside of each wire is covered with plastic. The plastic is called an **insulator**. Insulators do not conduct electricity. They keep electricity inside the wire.

Electricity comes into your house to the service panel. The service panel has many fuses.

An electrical current flows in a loop, called a **circuit**. Plug a lamp into an outlet and switch it on. The current flows continuously through wires, plug, cord, and bulb. The bulb lights up.

The current keeps flowing until the lamp is switched off. When the switch is turned off, it breaks the circuit. Then the bulb does not light.

Battery Power

A **battery** stores energy. Inside the battery are chemicals. When you connect a battery to a circuit, it makes electricity. The energy from a battery can light a flashlight. It can power a handheld game or a music player.

Batteries, like the ones in flashlights, make electricity available wherever you go.

Electricity from a battery is carried in a circuit. Wires connect a battery to a bulb. Electrical current flows from the battery, through the bulb, and back to the battery. It keeps flowing through the circuit.

When the circuit is broken, the electrical flow stops. The bulb does not light up.

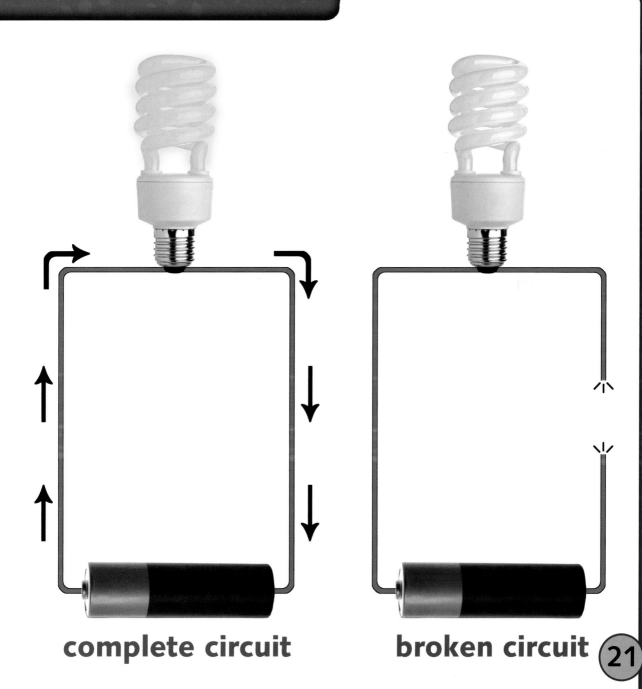

complete circuit   **broken circuit**

SHOW What You Know

1. How does electricity travel from a power plant?

2. What are some of the ways that electricity helps people work?

3. Why will a bulb not light if a circuit is broken?

Glossary

battery (BAT-uh-ree): a container that stores chemical energy that can produce electricity

circuit (SUR-kit): a complete path that an electrical current can flow around

conductors (kuhn-DUHK-turz): materials which electricity can travel through easily

electricity (i-lek-TRISS-uh-tee): a flow of charged particles that can be made from wind, solar, water, and fuel energy

energy (EN-ur-jee): the ability to do work

insulator (IN-suh-late-er): material that stops the flow of electricity

power lines (POW-er linez): metal cables or wires that conduct electricity from a power plant

work (wurk): transfer of mechanical energy from one thing to another

Index

Websites

www.bbc.co.uk/schools/scienceclips/ages/6_7/electricity.shtml

www.colorado.edu/physics/2000/waves_particles/wavpart2.html

www.eia.doe.gov/kids

www.miamisci.org/af/sln/frankenstein/www.mos.org/sln/toe/toe

www.mos.org/sln/toe/kite.html

About the Author

Buffy Silverman gets a charge out of learning about science. She writes about nature and science from her home in Michigan.